The Divine Romance with Jesus

We are All So Loved

Another Devotional Book with Selected Thoughts from the Song of Solomon and Others

By Eleanor Isaacson

Eleanor Isaacson Publications
www.eleanorisaacson.com

978-0-9991374-3-7 Print
978-0-9991374-4-4 ebook

Book and E-book designed and formatted by EBook Listing Services www.ebooklistingservices.com

Cover designed by Eleanora Elo
www.99designs.com

The Divine Romance with Jesus

We are All So Loved

DEDICATION

I dedicate this book to my new friend, Loraine.

God has brought her into my path during one of the Bible studies I was teaching. She came forward to tell me that our backgrounds were so similar.

We connected almost instantly and we now call each other "sis," because we help each other in every way.

We share stories from our childhoods and even find similar situations which our parents experienced. We now laugh at it all.

Her mother lived through the Nazi Regime like I did. We talked about many of the events that took place, which her mother never shared with her.

I mentioned to her that many people never talk about the traumas they may have experienced during any war. Our talks helped her understand her mother better.

I want to thank you Loraine for your encouragement in all I do, and for taking such good care of my dog when I need to be away.

I wish you all the blessings from our Lord in your life, and I thank Him for having connected us to Himself and to each other. You are one of His angels.

Friends are God's way of taking care of us!

May your kindness, goodness and faithfulness to so many people, come back to you as you travel on in your journey with the Lord Jesus Christ.

Table of Contents

Do You Want to Know God? 1
Kisses of His Mouth 5
Draw Me, We 8
His Banqueting House 10
His Treasures of Darkness 13
The Potter's Wheel 15
In His Arms 18
Walk By Faith 21
Looking Through the Lattice 24
The Bible In Our Hands 27
The Bible is a Simple Book 30
Arise, My Beautiful One, and Come Away 33
My Dove 36
The Little Foxes 38
My Beloved 41
She Lost the Sense of His Presence 44
He Describes Her Beauty 47
A Garden Enclosed 49
Awake, North Wind 51
He Comes Into Our Garden 53
He Knocks on Our Door 56
His Mouth Is Most Sweet 59
Now People Want Him Too 61
She is Now Back in His Arms 64
She Was His One and Only 67

Solomon Wrote the Book of Ecclesiastes....70
His Desire is For Me....73
Up From the Wilderness....75
A Double Portion....78
You Are His Jewel....81
Peter Did Walk On Water....84
Abraham and Lot....86
Believers Will Be Caught Up in the Rapture....88
The Bible Is a Trinity....91
How to Evangelize....93
The "U" In Jesus....96
Ten Lepers Healed... Only One Made Whole....98
Jesus Was Tempted By the Devil....101
Clouds....104
Confront Your Abusers....106
Widowhood....109
Be a Vibrant Senior....112
The Three Widows....115
Thoughts to Ponder by Eleanor....117
Created and Born....127
Cain and Abel....130
Sports: Acceptable Aggression and Violence....132
Being Single....135
The Altars of God....138
The Next Time You Feel Like God Can't Use You....141
Joseph in Prison....144
God's Two Tablets....146

The Burning Bush 148
I and My Father are One 151
They Saw His Nail-Pierced Hands 154
You are Worth It 157
Moses Broke the Ten Commandments 159
God is Lonely Without You 162
More Than a Conqueror 164
This Brings the Book to a Close 166

About the Author 167
Books by Eleanor 168
Invite Eleanor to Speak 171

Foreword

There are so many devotionals on the market today...so why another one?

Some of these devotionals sometimes tell us what to do, and how to live as Children of God. How do we become Children of God? We believe that the Lord Jesus Christ died for our sins on Calvary's Cross. He paid the penalty for each one of us. When we take that truth into our lives personally, then we become the Children of God. John 3:16...

> For God so loved the World that He gave His only begotten son, that WHOSOEVER believes in Him shall not perish but have everlasting life.
>
> —John 3:16

This verse has become my Spiritual Birth Certificate. I put my name into the WHOSOEVER space, February 25, 1954, 8:45 am and it was a Thursday.

Yes, we can now address God as our Father as children loved by Him. But there needs to come a time in our Christian walk when we must grow up into Him and become sons and daughters.

> ...as many as believed Him to them He gave the Power to become Sons, even to them who believe on His name"
>
> —John 1:12

Jesus goes even a step further and calls us His Beloved Bride, as we read in the book of the Song of Solomon. As a Bride, we need to stop praying like a needy baby talking to Papa....give me, give me, give me, but we need to pray like a grown up, mature in our faith and asking God as a Beloved Bride.

So this book hopefully will help us all "grow up into Him in all things." (Ephesians 4:15-16)

We can begin to enjoy the Lord's presence not as a religion, but as a Divine Romance with Jesus.

Introduction

How can anyone call Christianity a religion, when it is a Divine Romance between the Creator and His redeemed people?

It is not by coincidence that The Song of Solomon is in the center of the Bible, because romance is at the center of God's Heart. Not too many preachers and teachers talk about it. It is so intimate and sacred.

So come with me and together let's enter this sacred place and discover some nuggets to encourage us in our daily lives....

God loves us so much, with such deep passion, that our finite minds can't comprehend it or even imagine it. So He had to make a man and a woman to help us understand it!

The passion that exists between a newly married couple on their honeymoon is just a small picture of the passion God has for each of us spiritually. This truth should change our devotion time from one of duty to excitement and anticipation..."Oh what words of love will He tell me this morning?"

So let's begin.....

Do You Want to Know God?

When you think about it, all belief systems including atheism teach that humans can, by their own efforts, work hard to become worthy to be with God (or to become a good person).

The only belief system that contradicts this idea of the inherent goodness of people is the system centering around Jesus Christ. So right there, since it stands alone, it's worth understanding how and why being a believer is so different from all other systems.

God is unimaginably Holy and Perfect. No human can possibly be "good enough" to be with Him.

> For all have sinned, and fall short of the glory of God.
>
> —Romans 3:23

No matter how hard you try to be “worthy” (however that looks to you) you will never be able to do this perfectly. If you break God's moral law only one time that is enough to separate you permanently. Have you ever stolen anything, even something small? Have you ever lied? Have you ever pursued something or someone that didn't belong to you?

> For whoever keeps the whole law but fails in one point has become guilty of all of it.
>
> —James 2:10

However there is Good News! God is also infinitely Love... He IS love, not just HAS love. He deeply longs for each person to be reconciled to Himself, and therefore makes a way.

> For the wages of sin is death, but the free gift of God is eternal life in Christ Jesus our Lord.
>
> —Romans 6:23

The cornerstone of belief in Jesus is John 3:16:

> For God so loved the world, that he gave his only begotten Son, that whoever believes in him shall not perish but have eternal life.
>
> —John 3:16

Who is Jesus?

He was a real person, a Jewish man born of the line of Abrahan, Judah and David, who lived and died in Israel in the first century A.D.

Believers in Jesus also say he is the Son of God, God's perfect sacrificial lamb. Jesus lived without sin and freely offered his life so that through His sacrifice, we might be saved from condemnation and declared righteous and cleansed from sin before a holy God.

When you trust that Jesus paid the price for your sins, you can be reconciled to God:

> There is therefore now no condemnation for those who are in Christ Jesus...
>
> —Romans 8:1

God simply wants you to turn to Him and humbly trust him Him rather than trying to do it yourself. If you want to follow Him your words don't matter so much as your attitude. You can pray something like this:

*Lord Jesus, I want to know You personally. Thank You for dying on the cross for my sins. I open the door of my life and receive You as my Savior and Lord. Thank You for forgiving me of my sins and giving me eternal life. Take control of the throne of my life. Make me the kind of person You want me to be.**

*prayer from Bill Bright's *The Four Spiritual Laws*
(http://www.umich.edu/~mpactmov/4laws.htm)

> If you confess with your mouth that Jesus is Lord and believe in your heart that God raised him from the dead, you will be saved.
>
> —Romans 10:9

If you have prayed that prayer, you are in! Ask God to guide you as you learn more about Him.

Read your Bible starting with the book of John—this is the fourth book in the New Testament.

Find other believers.

Feel free to write to me at edi14@verizon.net if you have questions.

Welcome to the family!

So What Do You Think?

Kisses of His Mouth

> Let Him kiss me with the kisses of His mouth...
>
> —Song of Solomon 1:2

How intimate! Why does this verse not just describe Him kissing her with the kisses of his lips? Wouldn't that be less sexual and more prim and proper?

But No! Kisses on the mouth in this verse implies a total penetration of love through the kiss.

That is exactly what Jesus wants with us....total penetration of every part of our lives. An openness to our most innermost beings. Nothing hidden from him.

I find it interesting that when a new believer begins a life of total surrender to the Lord, the first thing the Lord will do is "have a garage sale" of our lives. He needs a clean vessel. He gets rid of baggage from the past, the old life, and wants us to pack fresh luggage so we can move forward with Him, in His power and strength, and begin a life of Romance with Him.

Baggage is things you think about from your past, abuses, neglect, rejection or failures. So what sort of baggage are you carrying around today?

Baggage can suck the energy out of you for years. If there were failures, read this:

> ...there is therefore NOW no condemnation to them who are in Christ Jesus, who walk not after the flesh, but after the spirit.
>
> —Romans 8:1

You are forgiven by God! Forgive yourself and move on! Jesus paid a heavy price when He died on the cross for you. He wants to love you, bless and cherish you, like a new groom on the honeymoon.

Accept His love and passionate embrace today and enjoy being His Bride.

So What Do You Think?

Draw Me, We

Draw me, we will run after you.

—Song of Solomon 1:4

Interesting! When the Lord draws us close to Himself and we obey, others will want to come with us in our walk with the Lord. People will see a love, a peace and freedom in us that will make them want it also in their lives.

Yes, Jesus said "you are the salt and the light" (Matt 5:13-16), and neither of those things make any noise. They are just an influence, a very powerful influence. We believers in Jesus Christ need to take this verse literally, and believe that we do make an impact, and an influence on our environment even if we don't think so.

So what kind of an impact and influence are you making in this world? Is Christ shining through you or are you just like everybody else...struggling, down, sad and settling into the negative atmosphere around you? Do you live by the news on your TV every day?

Spending time in prayer and reading the Bible will show in your life, your attitude and your outlook. People will see the peace in your face....you will shine for Jesus!

So What Do You Think?

His Banqueting House

> He brought me to the banqueting house, and His banner over me is love.
>
> —Song of Solomon 2:4

A Banquet

A banquet is a place where there is lots of food, celebration and crowds.

The Lord feeds us with His Word, the Bible, in private. He takes us away from the crowds to get us alone with Him. We need to read the Bible daily and spend time alone in His presence with praise and adoration.

We also need to spend time with other believers who are walking with the Lord. This is very important. A new believer is like a new born baby. It needs lots of food, love, care and being nurtured regularly. So it is with a new believer!

We must attend a church where the Bible is preached, and we need to choose our friends wisely, people who can help us grow in our faith.

A House

A house has many rooms and a basement where not much activity takes place. Let's assume that the Lord gives you a tour of this place and He stops in the basement, with no lights, no windows and no furniture. It is a dark place, and suddenly very silent. You can no longer sense Him.

Don't leave me! you cry. But there is a smile in Jesus' voice as he tells you that He will never leave nor forsake you (Hebrews 13:5).

He wants to teach you that you are to walk with Him by FAITH not sight. (2 Corinthians 5:7).

He tells you that He knows this is hard, but He wants you to trust Him, even in the dark times of your life. There are treasures to be had in the dark times.

> I will give you the treasures of darkness and the hoards in secret places that you may know that it is I, the Lord, the God of Israel, who call you by your name.
>
> —Isaiah 45:3

<u>His Banner over Me is Love</u> -

What I love about Song of Solomon 2:4 is the part about..."His banner over me is love."

So my friend, when the dark times come into our lives, remember that it is all about His great love for you. It is a banner, which means you can see it and read it all the time to remind you that it is so. What a caring God we have.

He has given us the Bible filled with 7,487 promises. We should never doubt or worry when our lives seem to fall apart, but choose to trust Him every day in every situation.

So What Do You Think?

His Treasures of Darkness

> I will give you the treasures of darkness, and hidden riches of secret places, that you may know that I, the Lord, which calls you by your name, am the God of Israel.
>
> —Isaiah 45:3

What kinds of treasures could possibly be in the dark times of our lives? Interesting! Do we ever look for the treasures? If we begin to do that, we will find lots of growth taking place in our faith walk. We are more into our daily Bible reading, more prayer, more trust and less being occupied with the actual problems we are facing.

Oh, the secret places of our lives we keep hidden, not only from ourselves but from others, is what the Lord will bring forward in our lives to heal us from them, or to show us that what we thought was abuse, neglect, rejection and the loneliness was actually tools in His Hands to shape us into spiritual people.

God wants to mold us into a vessel which He can use in His Kingdom. He puts us on a potter's wheel and spins it until the vessel He designed, is what He wants. (Jeremiah 18:1-6)

Examine the life of Joseph, in the book of Genesis chapters 37-50. Joseph was hated by his brothers, but God used it all to get him to Egypt, to be the Prime Minister, and ultimately to bring his family to Egypt, to feed them and forgive them. His life is a wonderful prediction and foreshadowing of our Lord Jesus Christ.

So my friend, look for the treasures in your darkness today. I know you will find them as He promised.

So What Do You Think?

The Potter's Wheel

> He said to Jeremiah, "Arise and go down to the potter's house, and there I will cause you to hear my words...cannot I do with you as this potter? Behold, as the clay is in the potter's hand, so are you in my hand."
>
> —Jeremiah 18:1-6

God must mold us, chisel us and crush us before we will submit to His will in our lives, before He can really use us in His service.

We are all born with a stubborn will, bold ego and an attitude of "I'm the best." So He gently chips away, through circumstances, until we realize that we are really not such hot stuff.

The potter's wheel is ruthless in the hands of our loving God, and if there are any lumps, He stops the wheel and starts over. We think of difficult circumstances in our lives are to hurt us, when actually they are to mold us into His likeness.

That is why I think, it is easier to serve the Lord as one gets older. It seems like we get smart enough to know, that His ways are always the best and for our good. The ego calms down and gets out of the way and we just let Him have His way with us. We surrender to His will in every situation.

Circumstances which aggravate us, along with toxic people, both in our families and friends, are actually tools in the hands of the Lord to force us to rest wholeheartedly trust in Him. It is not easy, but God has a wonderful purpose in our lives and this is a part of it.

So my friend, if you are on the potter's wheel today, just settle in and rest in His loving hands. Force yourself to trust Him and love what is happening in your life.

Study the Bible daily and use your concordance to look up verses that apply to your situation.

And if you are feeling particularly in need of inspiration listen to Esther Kerr Rusthoi's hymn *It Will Be Worth It All When We See Jesus*. This is a great song as you begin the day.

Hang in there!

So What Do You Think?

In His Arms

> His left hand is under my head, and His right hand embraces me.
>
> —Song of Solomon 2:6

Talk about romance. Hust think how intimate, private and romantic this verse is!

When lovers on their honeymoon are in each other's arms, nothing else matters at that moment, only each other. So it can be with us, when we believe and enjoy His Divine Love for us!

Just think how close the Lord really is to you, at this moment. It should be perfect rest and peace. All the noise and frustrations that surrounds us, really are not important. We are in His arms and all is at peace!

If you are widowed and loneliness is your daily dose of existence, dwell on this verse and tell the devil to get out of your thoughts:

> Submit yourselves therefore to God. Resist the devil, and he will flee from you.
>
> —James 4:7

Remember that most great people in the world have been lonely. During that time they invented great things which profited all of us. Even Joseph, after being sold by his brothers, was in a prison for thirteen years. During that time, he was prepared by God to be the Prime Minister of Egypt to save his family and the world from starvation. (Genesis 37, 39-41).

So use this lonely time for spiritual growth with your Heavenly Lover and He will use it to draw you closer to Him. It is a choice we must make. We must submit to God and let Him love us. Believe this verse and literally picture yourself in His strong embrace with you.

I am widowed 30 years as I write this, and I can honestly tell you, that this verse has shaped me into Being His Beloved Bride.

I serve the Lord more now than ever in my life, since my husband passed into the presence of the Lord in 1993.

So, will you flip your loneliness over into the Arms of your Heavenly Lover?

Make it personal and your loneliness will flee away like fog at sunrise.

So What Do You Think?

Walk by Faith

> I opened to my beloved, but my beloved had turned and gone. My soul failed me when he spoke. I sought him, but found him not; I called him, but he gave no answer.
>
> —Song of Solomon 5:6

So why does your beloved withdraw the sense of His presence from you? ,

Maybe it is to help you to walk by faith and not by sight and feelings. Jesus wants you to know that we are always in His embrace, even if we don't feel it. The walk of faith is one of trust and believing His Word.

> ...I will never leave you nor forsake you.
>
> —Hebrews 13:5

This is an important point in our Christian Walk—to know that the Bible promises are true, and that we can rest on them by believing all of the promises.

Remember that Jesus marveled at two thing in the New Testament—Great Faith (Luke 7:9) and Great Unbelief (Mark 6:6).

So where do you stand today with the Lord—Great Faith or Great Unbelief?

The more we are in His loving embrace, the easier it will become to just believe Him, in every way. When the hard times come, just to know His love will use it all to draw us close to Himself. So my friend, we can rest assured in His dealings with us.

Open your guarded heart today in exchange for the power of His love, which is as consistent as oxygen, as near as your heartbeat, and as defining as your fingerprints. He knows you, He made you and loves you like a bridegroom.

So What Do You Think?

Looking Through the Lattice

> My beloved is like a roe or a young hart. Behold, he stands behind our wall, gazing through the windows, looking through the lattice.
>
> —Song of Solomon 2:9

Our Lord always shows Himself through the lattice in all our situations.

A lattice is a screen which only partially shows what is behind it. So He stands behind every event that comes into our lives, not showing us His plan, but He peeks through our pain and tells us through His Word "I will never leave you nor forsake you." (Hebrews 13:5).

He gently forces us to lean, trust, believe and know that His plan for us must include testings and trials to help us to grow in faith.

Also, "looking through the lattice" can refer to all the stories of the Old Testament that foreshadow the Lord Jesus Christ.

For example, the lives of Noah, Abraham, Isaac, Jacob, Joseph, Moses, Boaz and all the others, give us a glimpse of what the life of Jesus will be like in the New Testament when He comes to earth.

The life of Joseph in the book of Genesis is almost a perfect prediction of what would happen to Jesus, in that He was rejected by His brothers, (the Jewish people), hated and put into a hole (a grave) but He came up and out of there. Joseph became the Ruler of

Egypt, and for Jesus that will happen in the future when He returns to set up His Kingdom on earth.

You might want to take a look at all the others in the Bible and see how their lives may be metaphors that fit into the predictions of Jesus Christ in the New Testament. Make it a part of your daily devotions.

Jesus shows Himself through the whole Old Testament, peeking through all the characters and events. So the Old Testament and the New are really one book. The Old Testament is the foundation for the New. The Old Testament predicts the coming of Messiah, the Lord Jesus Christ. In The New Testament, we see the fullness of His life and ministry.

So What Do You Think?

The Bible In Our Hands

For in it the righteousness of God is revealed from faith for faith, as it is written, "The righteous shall live by faith."

—Romans 1:17

Now it is evident that no one is justified before God by the law, for "The righteous shall live by faith."

—Galatians 3:11

Did you ever wonder how we got our Bibles? Many people have given their lives for the truth of that wonderful Book.

Since most people were uneducated in times past, many of the artists in many countries painted pictures portraying stories of the Bible to help people understand.

Many churches and pastors set themselves up as experts of the Bible. The Pope ruled the world. It was a sin to read the Bible and people had to confess their sins.

It was until Martin Luther in 1517, who as a monk in the Catholic Church, and a professor at the University of Wittenberg, Germany, began reading the Bible.

The Catholic Church was selling forgiveness. If people paid so much money, they would be allowed to sin. The Pope claimed that the power to do this was from God bestowed upon him.

Martin Luther, while reading the Bible, was struck by the phrase in Romans 1:17 and Galatians 3:11 that "The Just Shall Live By

Faith." In 1517 he nailed 95 Theses or propositions for debate on the church door in Wittenberg. He stated that the Bible is the only central religious authority, and that men and women may reach salvation only by their faith in Jesus Christ, by what He accomplished on the Cross for us. All of our works and deeds count for nothing in salvation.

This restatement of the Christian faith started the Protestant Reformation and it spread throughout the world!

To this day we are still enjoying the freedom in Christ. People protested the teachings of the Catholic Church, and many Protestant denominations began to spring up.

We can all thank Martin Luther for having the courage to confront the Church. It is because of him that we can all have a Bible in our hands. Martin Luther also wrote the hymn, "A Mighty Fortress is our God."

We can grow in our faith by obeying the truths of the Bible without the Pope ruling our lives.

Of course Martin Luther was excommunicated from the Catholic Church. We pay a price for teaching the truth in any age!

So What Do You Think?

The Bible is a Simple Book

Your word is a lamp to my feet and a light to my path.

—Psalm 119:105

Are you sometimes intimidated by the length, depth, and meaning of the Bible, compiled into sixty-six books? Well you are not alone. I have good news for you today. The Bible is a very simple Book when it comes to growing in our faith.

Most of the words for growing in our faith have only six letters or less:

Pray	Ask	Sing	God	Lord
Kneel	Share	Tell	Seek	Wise
Trust	Obey	Self	Rest	Love
Serve	Spirit	Bible	Heart	Joy
Faith	Doubt	Lead	Go	Walk
Hell	Jesus	Truth	Hate	Anger
Study	Give	Speak	Angel	Satan
Think	Life	Way	Mercy	Stand
Guide	Saved	Beauty	Kiss	Arms
Glory	Peace	Thanks	Hear	Abba
Heal	Come	Wait	Do	Fear
Hope	Hand	Faint	Child	Bride

Savior	Praise	Strong	Heaven	Fight
Pardon	Redeem	Friend	Church	Dream
Pride	Mouth	Lead	Judge	Write
Eye	Feet	Hands	Lips	Run

Know	Arise	Bless	Prove	Look
Teach	Gifts	Repent	Cry	Wrath
Wisdom	Power	Belief	Preach	Riches
Holy	Light	Gospel	Commit	Abide

Learn	Able	Gentle	Strive	Godly
Divine	Nature	Virtue	Grace	Hearts
Humble	Proud	Suffer	Feed	Flesh

So my friend, you don't need a college education to read and understand the Bible. Just read it faithfully and obey what it says, and you will bear much fruit for the Lord. Abide (stay close) to Him.

> Abide in me, and I in you. As the branch cannot bear fruit by itself, unless it abides in the vine, neither can you, unless you abide in me.
>
> —John 15:4

So What Do You Think?

Arise, My Love, My Beautiful One, and Come Away

> My beloved speaks and says to me: "Arise, my love, my beautiful one, and come away..."
>
> —Song of Solomon 2:10

God is always moving us forward in our walk with Him. There is always something new to learn, not only about ourselves, but also about Him.

That is why the Christian Life is never one of boredom. Every day is a fresh new day, with lots of choices before us either for blessings or consequences.

We should never waste our energy thinking about our past, with its sad events. We should forgive the people that have hurt, us and making it all an important part of our spiritual growth process.

We are all handmade, which to me means that every event was planned for me by a loving Father God.

When He asks us to "come away with Him", that to me means, don't think or dwell on the past. It is a choice we make.

Filling our minds and hearts with the promises of Scripture, will help us trust, pray and obey more easily and quickly.

Also spending lots of time alone in His presence will help us realize that people and events are really not that important in the light of eternity.

All the things we may worry about today really won't matter that much one hundred years from today.

This is what I have tried to do all my life and now that I am 88, I see that it has all been true.

So What Do You Think?

My Dove

> O my dove, in the clefts of the rock, in the crannies of the cliff, let me see your face, let me hear your voice, for your voice is sweet, and your face is lovely.
>
> —Song of Solomon 2:14

The Lord thinks of us as a gentle dove and He treats us that way. How very special and loving that is to me.

The cleft of the rock and the secret places of the stairs, is the quiet and secret place of prayer. The Lord waits for us to enter this place daily and He delights to hear our praises and prayers. He considers it all "sweet."

We may cry out in anguish, but to Him it is all so sweet.

> For he knows our frame; he remembers that we are dust.
>
> —Psalm 103:14

As a father lovingly treats his young children, so the Lord treats us.

We tend to be hard on ourselves, but our Great and Loving Shepherd draws us and cuddles us to His loving breast and understands.

He knows how we struggle to be spiritual, and He loves it when we want to be close to Him. He wants us to seek His face.

How do we seek His face when He is always invisible and intangible? By faith we draw close in our spirit, and we are nurtured and nourished. It is with the eye of faith we do this.

So What Do You Think?

The Little Foxes

> Take us the foxes, the little foxes, that spoil the vines: for our vines have tender grapes.
>
> —Song of Solomon 2:15 (KJV)

It's the little things in life that can aggravate us. It's the little grain of sand in our shoes that can make walking painful and difficult. So it is in our lives.

We seem to be able to handle the big problems that come our way, but the little annoyances from toxic people is what can do us in.

So it is in our spiritual life. It's the little sins that can keep us from enjoying the Lord to the fullest. For example, in a marriage, it is the little unspoken things that happen in relationships that can ultimately lead to the divorce court.

It is so important to have an open communication at all times. What does open communication really mean in a practical way? The following is an example from my marriage. Bob and I had a great marriage for 18 years. We had no children. We were both 40 when we married and it was our first marriage for both of us.

For a few months after we said "I do," I suggested that on the first of every month, we would give each other a performance review, like employers do in a company. Bob and I were both business people. We would go out to dinner, hold hands across the table, and I would open the conversation with these words "...so, Bob, how can I do things better this month from the last one?"

He might say, "well, Sweets, don't stretch my socks by folding them into each other, but just lay them on top of each other." I told my laundry lady to do this. She came once a week to clean and do laundry.

I said, "fine, anything else?"

People don't always feel comfortable to bring up the little things when they happen. But to have a specific time and place on the first of each month, without any emotions, makes both partners comfortable to bring up little annoyances.

After six months, we did not need to do this any longer. It really got our marriage off to a great start. Open and honest communication in any relationship is not only healthy, but both partners grow into each other and will enjoy life together so much more. So how many "little foxes" hide in your life today?

We need to keep a close a watch in our relationship with the Lord too. Satan is sneaky and subtle to keep us from spending time in the Word. So let's take charge of the "little foxes" that spoil our joy today.

So What Do You Think?

My Beloved

My beloved is mine, and I am His.

—Song of Solomon 2:16

In this verse, she is so satisfied with His love and goodness and has so settled into belonging to Him, that nothing at all matters. She is dead to the world. We can just hear her say these words. "Ah, I belong to Him totally."

She feels secure in this love relationship with her heavenly bridegroom. It seems like nothing seems more important at this moment.

She forgets her past, good and bad, and just rests in this wonderful, peaceful, and so fulfilling love.

We need to do that in our daily lives when we are in the presence of the Lord. We need to shut out all the past, all the noises, clutter and the to do lists, and just rest in our relationship with the Lord.

Jesus Christ paid a heavy price to make us His Bride when He died on the Cross of Calvary to pay for our sins.

Now that we are His beloved Bride, we need to focus on how much He loves us, and respond in a positive way. This will make life so much easier for us.

Rest is a weapon against our enemy, Satan, whose job it is to make us focus on our daily activities, and so rob us of the peace we can have in Him today.

"I belong to my beloved and He is mine." This relationship will last throughout the ages, today and into eternity.

If you are married with a very satisfying marriage, please remember that your husband, and all earthly relationships, are temporary. Your eternal husband, on the other hand, is eternal. He promises that He will never leave you nor forsake you (Hebrews 13:5).

We can read this verse backwards and forwards, and it means the same. It is called a Chiasmus.

So What Do You Think?

She Lost the Sense of His Presence

> On my bed by night I sought him whom my soul loves; I sought him, but found him not.
>
> —Song of Solomon 3:1

In chapter two of the Song of Solomon it seems she got so complacent and comfortable that she stopped seeking Him on a daily basis. It is called Backsliding! We let up on our daily spiritual discipline and just assume that all is well.

Folks, there are no coffee breaks in our walk with the Lord. We can lose the sense of His presence in a moment.

Satan's job is to make that happen by getting us so occupied with the things in our lives, and in the world, that we just don't have the time to focus, think, and live in His presence. It will take us some time to get back into close communion with our bridegroom by prayer, time in the Bible, meditation, and just focusing on who we are in Him, and how very much we are loved.

An example of this is found in Luke 2:44-46. Jesus was 12 years old when it was time to travel home from Jerusalem. However He was in the Temple asking questions of the Rabbis. It was probably His Bar Mitzvah. His parents, supposing Him to have been in the company traveling back went "one days' journey" before they realized that He wasn't among the group. It took Jesus' parents a "three days' journey" to find Him back in Jerusalem.

Drawing a parallel, it may take us one day to realize that we've lost the sense of our Lord's presence, but three days or more to get back into close fellowship with Him. It may take years or even a lifetime. Sometimes God will allow a crisis in our lives to push us back into fellowship with Him.

So What Do You Think?

He Describes Her Beauty

> You are altogether beautiful, my love; there is no flaw in you.
>
> —Song of Solomon 4:7 (NIV)

We may feel inadequate to be so loved, but His eyes only see beauty in us. When we are truly born again believers, we have His Righteousness and that is what He sees, not the flaws, failures and blemishes in our lives.

We learn that:

> There is therefore now no condemnation for those who are in Christ Jesus.
>
> —Romans 8:1

In the Song of Solomon He continues to tell her:

> You have captivated my heart, my sister, my bride; you have captivated my heart with one glance of your eyes, with one jewel of your necklace.
>
> —Song of Solomon 4:9

He is so ravished by her beauty that she doesn't say a word in this fourth chapter. That is how we are all loved by our Lord, our spiritual bridegroom.

If you sometimes feel no one really loves or cares, just read and memorize these verses, and your emptiness and loneliness will vanish away.

So What Do You Think?

A Garden Enclosed

> A garden locked is my sister, my bride, a spring locked, a fountain sealed.
>
> —Song of Solomon 4:12

How precious! He keeps us all to Himself, like an enclosed garden where only He can come in.

Sometimes we may feel alone and isolated from people, and it may so grip us that we descend into deep anxiety and depression. Loneliness has a way of doing that to us.

But if we were to make it all a spiritual experience, we would rejoice in the fact that we are not alone, but we are enclosed by our beloved for a time. He wants to teach us some things that we could not learn in a crowd.

Notice that "the fountain is sealed." You may not have any ministry to others until you are "enclosed" for some time. This is so necessary in any servant of the Lord.

In His time, when we have learned to depend on Him alone for anything we do, then the time will come when our "fountain," our usefulness to others, will spring up into living waters and streams will flow into the lives of others.

I like the fact that He also considers His spouse, His bride, to be His sister. He respects her and treats her gently, like a young sister. All husbands should do this, and not take advantage or abuse their wives.

Anyway, The Song of Solomon is so beautiful and filled with so much love, no wonder that it is in the center of the Bible. That is what the Heart of God is all about.

So What Do You Think?

Awake North Wind

> Awake, O north wind, and come, O south wind! Blow upon my garden, let its spices flow. Let my beloved come to his garden, and eat its choicest fruits.
>
> —Song of Solomon 4:16

Since she was enclosed in the garden of His presence and rested there, she is now ready to share it all with the world. She also has learned that the invitation to her beloved is always welcome with her. She adds "Let my beloved come into His garden, and eat its choicest fruits."

Sometimes we believers can get so occupied with the spiritual fruit we are bearing, we can forget that fruit, to be worthy of the Master, must be produced only as we abide in the Vine.

Our focus must not be on what kind of fruit we are producing, but how faithfully we are abiding in the Vine.

So What Do You Think?

He Comes Into Our Garden

> I came to my garden, my sister, my bride.
>
> —Song of Solomon 5:1

He comes into our life, our garden, only by invitation. We must invite Him into our lives, every corner of it, for us to receive His blessing.

We read in the cornerstone verse of the Bible, John 3:16:

> For God so loved the world, that He gave His only begotten Son, that whosoever believes in Him shall not perish but have everlasting life.
>
> —John 3:16

When we put our name into the whosoever, and believe in our hearts that Jesus died for our sins, was buried and rose again for our justification, we become "born again believers." It is all very personal.

We have to believe and receive the gift of salvation from a loving God. We don't slide into salvation automatically. For me it was February 25th 1954, at 8:45 am and it was a Thursday. I celebrate my spiritual birthday every year. It was a turning point in my life. I made a choice to invite Jesus Christ into my heart and life on that day.

It is like walking down the street past a church. One the outside there is a sign over the door that says ALL ARE WELCOME, COME

ON IN. We go inside and there is another sign on the inside of the door saying HELLO, I HAVE BEEN WAITING FOR YOU.

> The Lord is not slow to fulfill his promise as some count slowness, but is patient toward you, not wishing that any should perish, but that all should reach repentance.
>
> —2 Peter 3:9

Yes, all should come to repentance. We need to come and receive His wonderful gift of Salvation.

Have you done that? If not, do it today. Put your name into John 3:16 in place of "whosoever" and begin a wonderful new Life.

So What Do You Think?

He Knocks on Our Door

> My beloved is knocking. "Open to me, my sister, my love, my dove, my perfect one..."
>
> —Song of Solomon 5:2-7

> Behold, I stand at the door and knock. If anyone hears my voice and opens the door, I will come in to him and eat with him, and he with me.
>
> —Revelation 3:20

Our Lord is always knocking at the door of our lives, and waits to be invited in.

Here in the Song of Solomon, she was again lazy and complacent in her love relationship with the Lord.

> I had put off my garment; how could I put it on? I had bathed my feet; how could I soil them?...
>
> I opened to my beloved, but my beloved had turned and gone. My soul failed me when he spoke. I sought him, but found him not; I called him, but he gave no answer.
>
> The watchmen found me as they went about in the city; they beat me, they bruised me, they took away my veil, those watchmen of the walls.
>
> —Song of Solomon 5: 3, 6-7

This section tells us that she didn't want to, but finally got out of bed and put on her coat to open the door. However, she finds that her beloved has withdrawn Himself and was gone. So she goes into the city looking for Him and the watchmen (the unbelieving people in the world) find her. They beat her up, wound her, and take away her veil.

This is an interesting concept, that when a believer gets away from walking with the Lord, the people in the world get angry with them and are very disappointed! The world expects believers to live a godly life, even though they themselves do not believe the Bible or trust in the Lord.

In Matthew Jesus said that you, the believer, are the SALT of the earth and the LIGHT of the world (Matthew 5:13-16).

Salt and light don't make any noise. They are simply an influence. So we do not always have to speak to shine for the Lord. Do you realize that we are an influence wherever we go, even though we may not know it?

When we walk closely with the Lord and spend time reading His Word, we will shine for Him. The light of His presence will shine through us. So my friend, go shine for Him today.

So What Do You Think?

His Mouth is Most Sweet

> His mouth is most sweet, and he is altogether desirable. This is my beloved and this is my friend, O daughters of Jerusalem.
>
> —Song of Solomon 5:16

Now she describes her beloved to the watchmen and the city people who beat her up, that her beloved is not only a beautiful person, but everything He says is most sweet.

His words are overflowing with love and grace towards her, even when she gets lazy, unresponsive to His love, and doesn't open the door, (to let Him into her life).

It is all of Grace! He loves us regardless of our past sins and lack of love towards Him today.

> We love Him because He first loved us.
>
> —I John 4:19

Let us enjoy His Sweet Words found in the Bible today and let us decide, that from this day forward, we will shine for Him.

So What Do You Think?

Now People Want Him Too

> Where has your beloved gone, O most beautiful among women? Where has your beloved turned, that we may seek him with you?
>
> —Song of Solomon 6:1

When we are restored to the Lord in fellowship with Him, our family and friends will want to have a relationship with Him also.

King David experienced the restoration of the Lord also:

> Restore to me the joy of your salvation, and uphold me with a willing spirit. Then I will teach transgressors your ways, and sinners will return to you.
>
> —Psalm 51:12-13

Peter in the New Testament denied our Lord Jesus Christ three times, as Jesus had predicted he would...

> Then they seized him and led him away, bringing him into the high priest's house, and Peter was following at a distance. And when they had kindled a fire in the middle of the courtyard and sat down together, Peter sat down among them. Then a servant girl, seeing him as he sat in the light and looking closely at him, said, "This man also was with him." But he denied it, saying, "Woman, I do not know him." And a little later someone else saw him and said, "You also are one of them." But Peter said, "Man, I am not." And after an interval of about an hour still another

> insisted, saying, "Certainly this man also was with him, for he too is a Galilean." But Peter said, "Man, I do not know what you are talking about." And immediately, while he was still speaking, the rooster crowed. And the Lord turned and looked at Peter. And Peter remembered the saying of the Lord, how he had said to him, "Before the rooster crows today, you will deny me three times." And he went out and wept bitterly.
>
> —Luke 22:54-62

However, Peter was wonderfully restored, as we read in John 21, after the resurrection of our Lord. The scene took place on the beach, after Peter was fishing all night and caught nothing. It was Jesus who told him to cast his net on the right side of the boat, and there were 153 fish in the net. Jesus then asked Peter three times if he loved him and each time Peter responded with a "yes, yes, yes Lord, you know that I love You."

When we get to the book of Acts 1:15-26, we see that it was Peter who became the first bold evangelist and spoke about Jesus being the Promised Messiah, and three thousand people listened to Peter intently and accepted Jesus Christ into their lives. Yes, Peter was restored and with fire and boldness preached the promise of salvation wherever he went.

So how about you? Have you fallen away from your heavenly Bridegroom a little? Well, come on back. He is waiting for you with open arms.

So What Do You Think?

SHE IS NOW BACK IN HIS ARMS

> I am my Beloved's and my Beloved is mine.
>
> —Song of Solomon 6:3

She is now more in love with Him than ever, after she was restored to her heavenly Bridegroom.

And so it is with us! Many times we will end up loving the Lord more after we have slipped away from close fellowship with Him.

This is what happened to King David. He sinned with Bathsheba and then killed her husband, as we read in 2 Samuel 11.

But David admitted his sin. He agreed with God about his sin, and did not argue about it by saying something like "I'm the King. I can do anything I want with any woman." No he repented and God restored him into close fellowship with Himself.

He writes about it in the Psalms:

> Against you, you only, have I sinned and done what is evil in your sight, so that you may be justified in your words and blameless in your judgment...
>
> Create in me a clean heart, O God, and renew a right[a] spirit within me. Cast me not away from your presence, and take not your Holy Spirit from me. Restore to me the joy of your salvation, and uphold me with a willing spirit.
>
> —Psalm 51:4, 10-12

And so it is with us. When we slip away and begin to realize how empty our lives are without Him, we need to confess our sin, and

God in His grace and faithfulness, will restore us and begin to use us more than ever before.

After King David was restored, he loved the Lord more and wrote most of his Psalms found in the Bible, especially Psalms 23, 32 and 51. Read them and be encouraged.

We will serve the Lord more fervently after we have been forgiven of our failures. This can be seen in many of the Patriarchs in the Bible, such as Moses, Jacob, David, Paul the Apostle, and Peter. Look them up in your Concordance and make their life's stories a part of your devotions.

So will it be with us. If you need to come clean with the Lord, do it today.

> If we say we have no sin, we deceive ourselves, and the truth is not in us. If we confess our sins, he is faithful and just to forgive us our sins and to cleanse us from all unrighteousness.
>
> —1 John 1:8-9

So What Do You Think?

She Was His One and Only

> There are sixty queens and eighty concubines, and virgins without number. My dove, my perfect one, is the only one, the only one of her mother, pure to her who bore her.
>
> —Song of Solomon 6:8-9

King Solomon had many women at his disposal, as we see:

> Now King Solomon loved many foreign women, along with the daughter of Pharaoh: Moabite, Ammonite, Edomite, Sidonian, and Hittite women, from the nations concerning which the Lord had said to the people of Israel, "You shall not enter into marriage with them, neither shall they with you, for surely they will turn away your heart after their gods." Solomon clung to these in love. He had 700 wives, who were princesses, and 300 concubines. And his wives turned away his heart.
>
> —1 Kings 11:1-3

Despite all these women at his disposal, King Solomon mentions only one he loved, the woman he writes about in the Song of Solomon. All the other women were probably for convenience, for example to maintain peace with the neighboring nations by marrying many of the ruling king's daughters. Can you imagine how many children he must have fathered with all these women?

Where did Solomon learn this way of life to have more than one thousand wives and three-hundred concubines? I think he learned it from this dad, King David, who had thirty concubines, and eight wives. (2Samuel 3:2-5).

Sadly for David and Solomon, having many wives is not God's will. When Moses was laying out God's laws in the Torah he writes:

> [The king] shall not acquire many wives for himself, lest his heart turn away, nor shall he acquire for himself excessive silver and gold.
>
> —Deuteronomy 17:17

David didn't read this verse, but instead he let his lust rule his life, which ultimately brought sorrow.

Our actions matter, not just for us but for those who come after us. God's word also states:

> [The Lord] will by no means clear the guilty, visiting the iniquity of the fathers on the children and the children's children, to the third and the fourth generation.
>
> —Exodus 34:7

So Solomon learned polygamy from his dad, and it was multiplied in his life. Despite a promising beginning as ruler, and being the builder of God's Temple, at the end the women and other attractions caused Solomon to turn away from God.

We need to take our actions into consideration, when we become parents. Children learn by observation and not just what we say. Let's promise ourselves to be good examples to those who follow us.

So What Do You Think?

Solomon Wrote the Book of Ecclesiastes

> Vanity of vanities! All is vanity...there is nothing new under the sun...And I applied my heart to know wisdom and to know madness and folly. I perceived that this also is but a striving after wind.
>
> —Ecclesiastes 1:2, 9, 17

Solomon is disheartened with the ultimate insignificance of this world's attractions and challenges—all of them! He concludes:

> The end of the matter; all has been heard. Fear God and keep his commandments, for this is the whole duty of man.
>
> —Ecclesiastes 12:13

Of all the people in the Bible to write this book, Solomon is the best one to write it, because he had it all—wealth, wisdom, women, and prestige—but it was his lust that ultimately destroyed him.

In this book, he spells it all out for us and concludes that ALL IS VANITY!

The only satisfaction in life is to know God, and to do His Will. This will bring peace, joy and fulfillment. So there!

If you are trying to fill your life will all the things mentioned in this book, remember that, at the end of the book, Solomon tells us that it is all Vanity and vexation of spirit.

Let's learn from him today, and put the Lord first in our lives, and all other things God will give us, in His time, and when we are ready to receive them.

If you are single and think that all your joy would be complete if you only had a husband? Remember, Solomon had 1,300 women at his beck and call 24/7 and he says....All IS VANITY!

So What Do You Think?

His Desire is For Me

> I am my beloved's, and His desire is for me.
>
> —Song of Solomon 7:10

Yes, in every way, His desire is toward us. He proved it at the Cross of Calvary when he paid for our sins to win us to Himself and to make us His beloved Bride. Think of the price He paid to make us His own! We will never know what all of that involved. Praise and adoration should be our daily occupation.

The Lord is always thinking of us and plans our lives, with all its trials, to help us grow in faith. We read:

> He who began a good work in you will bring it to completion at the day of Jesus Christ.
>
> —Philippians 1:6

We should never fear, doubt or get discouraged when things don't go our way. GOD IS IN CONTROL and when we have placed our faith and trust in His Divine Love He works all things together for good (Romans 8:28).

What can possibly go wrong when you are in His arms? So, my friend, trust, trust, and trust some more in your Divine Bridegroom who loves you so much that He enables every event in your life to draw you closer to His bosom.

I am a Christian for 69 years at this point, and I am writing this for you to be encouraged. You are so loved, BELIEVE IT.

So What Do You Think?

Up From the Wilderness

> Who is that coming up from the wilderness, leaning on her beloved?
>
> —Song of Solomon 8:5

> Trust in the Lord with all your heart, and do not lean on your own understanding.
>
> —Proverbs 3:5

I so enjoy putting verses together, and I have done this all my life. Comparing Scripture with Scripture brings so much light on a subject.

I've done it here and this is how I read it—we are to lean upon our beloved and NOT on our own understanding.

So my friend, do you want to get up and out of a painful situation in your life? Then do what these two verses tell you. Lean Hard On Your Beloved and NOT On Your Own Understanding.

How do we do this? We need to trust in Him, who loves us SO MUCH that nothing bad can really happen to us. It is all sent to us by a loving Father who wants to strengthen our faith.

Let's face it, our faith really can't grow unless we are forced to trust in Him, read our Bibles consistently and let go of fear and self-effort. It is when we are faced with a situation in our lives that we just can't handle that we reach out to God.

It's like a parent who forces the baby to take the first steps alone. He will fall down, but the parent is right there to catch him.

So it is with our Heavenly Father. With each trial, we learn that His Everlasting Arms are Underneath us.

> The eternal God is your dwelling place, and underneath are the everlasting arms. And he thrust out the enemy before you and said, "Destroy."
>
> —Deuteronomy 33:27

So, my friend, lean hard.

So What Do You Think?

A Double Portion

The Lord is my portion...

—Psalm 119:57

...Please let there be a double portion of your spirit on me.

—2 Kings 2:9

The Lord is my chosen portion ...

—Psalm 16:5

...God is the strength of my heart and my portion forever.

—Psalm 73:26

"The Lord is my portion," says my soul, "therefore I will hope in him."

—Lamentations 3:24

But the Lord's portion is his people...

—Deuteronomy 32:9

Most Americans are on a diet some time in their lives. The message from all dietitians always seems to be "Smaller portions on your plate is the way to control your weight."

This is good advice when talking about food, but in spiritual terms it is not a good idea to go on a spiritual diet.

Isn't it good to know that we can't get too much of the presence of the Lord, His Word, as a part of our daily routine Bible study, and resting in His Loving Arms? It is okay to overeat on this heavenly food.

It was Elisha, in 2 Kings 2:9, who asked Elijah to give him a double portion of his spirit. God delights when we feed on His Word and grow in faith. He is also delighted when we come to Him in bold faith asking big things from Him.

But God has a portion in His heart too, and that is His people - you and me!

So What Do You Think?

YOU ARE HIS JEWEL

> They shall be mine, says the Lord of hosts, in the day when I make up my treasured possession...
>
> —Malachi 3:17

> For you yourselves are fully aware that the day of the Lord will come like a thief in the night.
>
> —Thessalonians 5:2

> You shall be a crown of beauty in the hand of the Lord, and a royal diadem in the hand of your God.
>
> —Isaiah 62:3

Have you ever considered yourself a royal diadem, a costly jewel? Think about how precious the Lord thinks you are to Him.

So, no matter how you feel about yourself, and what others may have told you in the past. Maybe you heard that you were not planned or wanted but you came along anyway. Maybe your teachers told you that you will never make it in math, or in any other subject for that matter. You may even have been sexually abused and told that unless you give sex to men, you will never really "be a woman of worth." One of the women I mentored was told this by her dad.

Well, whatever anybody said to you in the past, just think about how very special and precious you are to the Lord. He died for you to make you His, and no one on this planet is more important than the Creator Who made you for Himself.

When we read that He is a thief, what do thieves steal when they break into a home? They try to find the jewels first. Well our God will come for us as a thief in the night to snatch us away, to be with Himself for ever and ever.

How wonderful it is to be a Christian believer. Life is filled with wonder and excitement, and we have a glorious future ahead of us. We indeed have a blessed hope. The best is always just ahead. Be on the lookout for it!

So What Do You Think?

Peter Did Walk on Water

> He said, "Come." So Peter got out of the boat and walked on the water and came to Jesus. But when he saw the wind, he was afraid, and beginning to sink he cried out, "Lord, save me." Jesus immediately reached out his hand and took hold of him, saying to him, "O you of little faith, why did you doubt?"
>
> —Matthew 14:29-31

Peter did walk on the water, even it was just for a few seconds, and Jesus rebuked him when he began to sink. The reason he did not sink for those few seconds was because the words of Jesus Christ which are a strong foundation for all of us, no matter what we are walking or standing on. Actually, he walked on "the Word of God", which is solid ground.

Interesting that Jesus would rebuke Peter for sinking. This means that he could have walked if he would have kept his eyes on Jesus and not on what was going on around him.

So my fearful friend, your situation may feel like you are sinking, or that boisterous waters are shaking you up, or you are uncertain about the outcome and you feel all alone. Remember Jesus is right there with you pulling you up and out. Remember when your focus is on Him, you can do anything.

It was Paul the Apostle who said "I can do all things through Christ, who strengthens me" (Phillipians 4:13).

What a Savior we have!

So What Do You Think?

ABRAHAM AND LOT

> And the Lord appeared to him [Abraham] by the oaks of Mamre, as he sat at the door of his tent in the heat of the day...The Lord said, "I will surely return to you about this time next year, and Sarah your wife shall have a son."...The Lord said, "Shall I hide from Abraham what I am about to do..."
>
> —Genesis 18:1,10,17

> The two angels came to Sodom in the evening, and Lot was sitting in the gate of Sodom. When Lot saw them, he rose to meet them and bowed himself with his face to the earth...
>
> —Genesis 19:1

Interesting that the Lord Himself appeared unto Abraham, as we read in Genesis 18. But in chapter 19, he did not appear Himself, but sent two angels. Why?

I think it is because Abraham had a close personal relationship with the Lord, whereas Lot did not. He knew about the Lord, but had no close relationship with him. We see this in the life Lot lived in Sodom.

So my friend, which one of these men do you identify with today? Is it with Abraham, who had a very close walk with the Lord, or is it with Lot ,who just knew about the Lord?

It is one thing to know about the Lord and sit faithfully in your pew on Sundays. It is another thing to walk daily in close fellowship with Him.

So What Do You Think?

Believers Will Be Caught Up In The Rapture

> For the Lord himself will descend from heaven with a cry of command, with the voice of an archangel, and with the sound of the trumpet of God. And the dead in Christ will rise first. Then we who are alive, who are left, will be caught up together with them in the clouds to meet the Lord in the air, and so we will always be with the Lord. Therefore encourage one another with these words.
>
> —1 Thessalonians 4:16-18

It could happen today!

There are at least two views on the Rapture, the event in which Jesus snatches his Bride, the Church, into heaven to be with Him.

The first view is that it will happen when Jesus returns to put down all evil forces and rule and reign after the Tribulation. Proponents of this theory argue that the Rapture is not mentioned anywhere in the Old Testament nor in the four gospels.

I say, of course it isn't mentioned! The Rapture is about the Church. The Church didn't exist until Acts once Jesus had ascended back to Heaven.

The Old Testament describes the completion of the Law and the Prophets about the Messiah, and the gospels describe the revelation of the Messiah in one man, Jesus Christ. Jesus' statement in Matthew 16:18 that He WILL build His Church on Peter's declaration that Jesus is the Son of God is set in the future.

The Church is a Mystery (Ephesians 5:32). The Church Age is actually a parenthesis in God's dealings with the Nation of Israel, and the focus of God's attention will turn firmly back to the Jewish people in the Tribulation to get them to see Him, their Messiah. Yes, Gentiles are blessed to read the four Gospels, but the main point of them is to prove to Israel that Jesus is the Promised One. The Church doesn't exist until after Jesus is gone.

The second view on the Rapture is the one I happen to agree with, that the Rapture will happen BEFORE the Tribulation and Jesus returns to set up the Millennial Kingdom. It's hard for me to imagine otherwise. If the Rapture takes place at Jesus' triumphal return, would we be caught up and then make an immediate U turn and come back with Him?

Whichever view you think is correct, we can agree that Jesus is coming, and He's coming soon! If not in the Rapture, He will come for you when you die, and that could happen any time.

Are you ready?

So What Do You Think?

The Bible is a Trinity

In the Old Testament The Father/God is prominent.

In the four Gospels the Son is prominent.

In the book of Acts and the rest of the New Testament the Holy Spirit is prominent.

We are today living in the Book of Acts! The Book of Acts really has no closing to it. It ends with:

> ...proclaiming the kingdom of God and teaching about the Lord Jesus Christ with all boldness and without hindrance.
>
> —Acts 28:31

What I learn from this ending is that I am to do what it says, that is, preaching the Kingdom of God and teaching with confidence the Lord Jesus Christ everywhere I go.

So how about you. Are you doing that too?

So What Do You Think?

How to Evangelize

> And he said to them, "Go into all the world and proclaim the gospel to the whole creation."
>
> —Mark 16:15

> And he gave the apostles, the prophets, the evangelists, the shepherds and teachers, to equip the saints for the work of ministry, for building up the body of Christ.
>
> —Ephesians 4:11-12

> When I say unto the wicked, "You shall surely die", and you give him no warning, nor speak to warn the wicked from his wicked way, to save his life; the same wicked man shall die in his sin; but his blood will I require at your hand. But if you warn him and he turn not from his wickedness, nor from his wicked way, he shall die in his sin; but you have delivered your soul.
>
> —Ezekiel 3:18-19

Wow...this is heavy stuff!

So we see that evangelizing, telling people about the wonderful good news of the Gospel, is both a Gift from God, but it is also a great responsibility. It is a command from the Lord Himself.

To this day I have always taken the verse from Ezekiel literally. I make opportunities to witness and share my faith with people wherever I go.

The Lord always seems to open doors for me to do that. He will do the same for you.

It was St. Francis of Assisi, a Catholic monk, who was born in Italy in 1182, who said many years ago "I preach the Gospel every day and sometimes I use words."

It is our life that really does the talking. When we enjoy the Lord in our lives so much, it will show on our faces. The Holy Spirit, Who lives within us when we have trusted Jesus Christ as our Savior, will shine through us.

We have a responsibility to share our faith with people and bring them to a knowledge of our Lord Jesus Christ. All we need to do is just tell people what the Lord is doing in our lives. Of course, we need to walk closely with Him on a daily basis.

So, do you need to win your friends and family members to the Lord? Just live before them, and they will someday ask you for the peace, joy and purpose in your life that makes you so happy, positive and carefree!

So What Do You Think?

THE "U" IN JESUS

Before U were thought of or time had begun
God even stuck U in the name of His Son
And each time U pray, you'll see it is true
You can't spell out JesUs and not include U.

You're a pretty big part of His wonderful name,
For U, He was born, that's why He came
And His great love for U is the reason He died,
It even takes U to spell crUcified.

Isn't it thrilling and splendidly grand
He rose from the dead, with U in His plan
The stone rolled away, the gold TrUmpet blew,
And this word resUrrection is spelled with a U.

So many great people are spelled with a U
Don't they have a right to know JesUs too?
It all depends now on what U will do,
He'd like them to know, but it all starts with "U"

So let's all get busy gossiping the Gospel!

So What Do You Think?

Ten Lepers Healed... Only One Made Whole

> And as he entered a village, he was met by ten lepers, who stood at a distance and lifted up their voices, saying, "Jesus, Master, have mercy on us." When he saw them he said to them, "Go and show yourselves to the priests." And as they went they were cleansed. Then one of them, when he saw that he was healed, turned back, praising God with a loud voice; and he fell on his face at Jesus' feet, giving him thanks. Now he was a Samaritan. Then Jesus answered, "Were not ten cleansed? Where are the nine? Was no one found to return and give praise to God except this foreigner?" And he said to him, "Rise and go your way; your faith has made you well."
>
> —Luke 17:12-19

So where were the nine lepers that were healed, as they went to show themselves to the priests in the Temple? They were thankless and unappreciative, just like some people today!

Are we really thankful to God for all His blessings to us daily? We have good health (even if we hurt here and there), enough food to eat (I experienced a starvation period when I lived in Germany after the WWII in Germany), relatively peace in our country, a roof over our heads, cars to drive to take us wherever we want to go, open Bibles on our laps, and churches to attend without fear. We are indeed blessed, especially compared to believers in other countries.

Being thankful to the Lord at all times is the key to a fulfilling and satisfying life.

The above verse is interesting. The ten lepers were healed, but only one returned to give thanks to the Lord. He was not only healed, but he was made "whole."

Why? He went to the "Real Priest," the Lord Jesus Christ. Jesus will do the same for us! Jesus is not so interested in giving us healing for a specific problem. No, He wants to heal us in every way, body, soul and spirit.

So my friend, give your life totally to Him, and you will see what God will do for you in every area of your life.

Are you only healed or completely made "whole?"

So What Do You Think?

Jesus was Tempted by the Devil

> And when Jesus was baptized, immediately he went up from the water, and behold, the heavens were opened to him, and he saw the Spirit of God descending like a dove and coming to rest on him; and behold, a voice from heaven said, "This is my beloved Son, with whom I am well pleased." Then Jesus was led up by the Spirit into the wilderness to be tempted by the devil.
>
> —Matthew 3:16-17, 4:1

These three verses are together in the narrative, with a chapter division added later. When we connect them we see that Jesus was led by the Spirit into the wilderness, to be tempted by the devil BECAUSE God was pleased with Him.

How encouraging this is for us to connect these verses in our lives too. When we are tested and tried by the devil, is it also because God is pleased with us, His blood bought children?

He wants to teach us not only to use the Bible promises against the devil, like Jesus did, but He wants us to grow in faith. How else will we learn to trust our loving heavenly Father unless our faith is tested also?

He also wants to teach us that we, as believers, have the authority over the evil one, and when we "submit to God, resist the devil and he will flee from you" (James 4:7).

There are a lot of flees in the Bible, with 101 mentions in the verses in the Bible.

So my friend, if you are in the thick wilderness right now in your life, remember that God is with you, and will get you up and out in His time.

Trust and trust and trust some more. Double up on your time with the Lord in your Bible, study and know that you are so loved. He is using this hard time to develop your faith.

So What Do You Think?

CLOUDS

> And when [Jesus] had said these things, as they were looking on, he was lifted up, and a cloud took him out of their sight.
>
> —Acts 1:9

When we think of clouds, we think of impending rain or a storm, always something negative. But in the Bible, clouds always symbolize God's Divine Presence.

In the Old Testament, clouds were a shade against the heat or burning desert sun. The cloud in the wilderness over the Tabernacle, was God's way of letting the Israelites know that He was with them. When the cloud moved, it was their signal to pack up and move wherever the cloud moved (Ex 40:36). It was a cloud by day and fire by night. The cloud of God's glory filled the temple at its dedication (1 kings 8:10-11, 2 Chronicles 5:14).

In the New Testament, our Lord Jesus Christ was taken up in a cloud right in front of the disciples' eyes. They actually saw Him go up!

Most exciting for us is that we will one day see the clouds of God's Divine Presence for ourselves, when our Lord Jesus comes back just as He left—in a cloud.

Is your life cloudy today? God's Presence is right there with you in your cloudy day bringing you His blessings.

So What Do You Think?

Confront Your Abusers

> Then David said to the Philistine, "You [Goliath] come to me with a sword and with a spear and with a javelin, but I come to you in the name of the Lord of hosts, the God of the armies of Israel, whom you have defied. This day the Lord will deliver you into my hand, and I will strike you down and cut off your head...
>
> —1 Samuel 17:45-46

> Rather, speaking the truth in love, we are to grow up in every way into him who is the head, into Christ.
>
> —Ephesians 4:15

There is a relief and freedom when we can confront an abuser with forgiveness in love.

After the first word comes out of our mouths, it seems that we have instantly grown up into adulthood! I did this with my mother and father. If we never get to do this, we will forever be a victim, not only to our abuser, but to all people we come in contact with. We will forever have a victim mentality, and our posture, self esteem, conversation and behavior will display it. People will sense this, and take advantage of it.

We will also always attract people who will victimize us. If a girl was abused by her dad, she will probably be attracted to a man, and marry him, who will be like her dad, abusive.

However, if she gets the courage as an adult and confront her dad, and what he did to her when she was young, this confrontation, as an adult, will help her in her future relationships. No more abuse from anyone in this world, will be her new attitude.

King David, at the age seventeen, did this and as he spoke the words of confidence to the giant Goliath, he almost instantly rose to his anointed kingship. After he slew Goliath, his brothers never again treated him like a victim.

So, we cannot really reach our full mature adulthood, until we have confronted our abusers, either abuse in our past, or in our present relationships.

Once we have addressed, loved, forgave the people who hurt us, we become strong in other areas of our lives also, including toxic people who are present in our daily lies. Try it, and God will help you, give you courage, and the wisdom to do it in love and forgiveness. You will grow up into Him in all things.

So What Do You Think?

Widowhood

[God is the] Father of the fatherless and protector of widows...

—Psalm 68:5

And let the widows trust in Me, says the Lord,

—Jeremiah 49:11

There is a life for us after we walk away from a cemetery and a covered grave. It is a new life now, only different! Psychologists tell us that widowhood is the most serious and stressful time in our lives. Our identity was being someone's mate. Suddenly, we are one in a world of twos.

How can we handle it all in a positive way? First, we must allow a period of grief. We stare at the photos and remember the good old times. We have crying moments throughout the day.

This is all normal but we cannot choose to live in that mode forever. There has to come a time when we say to ourselves, Enough!

If you have a personal relationship with the Lord, and I hope you do, this will help.

But if not, now would be a good time to get started to create a relationship with Jesus Christ by opening your heart to Him. He died on the cross of Calvary to pay for your sins, and wants to give you a whole new life. He is now your Husband, (your Mate), as we read in Isaiah 54:5.

Ask and trust Him to lead you into a new life now as a single. Let it make you into a spiritual person. Double up on your prayer time and Bible study. Seek people who will encourage you in this new life

Thank God all the time, even for the pain and emptiness, He will fill it! Be open with God about your pain. Remember with God in your life, the best is always ahead of you.

So What Do You Think?

Be a Vibrant Senior

> So even to old age and gray hairs, O God, do not forsake me, until I proclaim your might to another generation, your power to all those to come.
>
> —Psalm 71:18

> They are planted in the house of the Lord; they flourish in the courts of our God. They still bear fruit in old age...
>
> —Psalm 92:13-14

> And even to your old age I am He, and to gray hairs I will carry you. I have made, and I will bear; I will carry and will save.
>
> —Isaiah 46:4

What wonderful promises from our God to seniors. Some of the most productive years are the senior years, depending on how you lived getting there. So you think your life is over once you have blown out seventy candles on your birthday cake. You feel you have come to the last gas station in your life. Well my friend, just refuel and keep on keeping on! It is all about your attitude!

I am no longer a Teen-ager, but a Seen-ager. I've seen a lot and now I have everything I wanted when I was a teen, only fifty years later.

I don't have to go to school anymore, unless I want to.

I get an allowance every month from Uncle Sam, not my dad.

I don't have any more curfews, I can come home when I want.

Brains of older people are slower because they know so much.

All this information in the brain puts pressure on the ears, so hard of hearing is the result.

Walking into a room and forgetting why you came in there is not a memory problem. It is nature's way of making you get more exercise!

What can you do if you're in your golden years? Lots of things! Read a book a week, watch less TV, be open to new adventures, go to college, work puzzles, write your life story, always put God first in all you do, be thankful and grateful for every day of your life.

You are so loved by God. Believe it. Maintain a good posture, be well groomed at all times even when you are home alone, walk one mile a day, eat smaller frequent meals, be outgoing, continue dreaming of your future, get rid of everything that isn't useful, do the things that make you feel beautiful and joyful.

All that really matters in the end is to know that you are so loved by God, and nothing is really more important.

So What Do You Think?

The Three Widows

> Then they lifted up their voices and wept again. And Orpah kissed her mother-in-law [Naomi], but Ruth clung to her.
>
> —Ruth 1:14

These 3 widows represent all of humanity!

Naomi's two sons married foreign brides, Orpah and Ruth.

Orpah represents the ones who hear but do not follow. She heard about the blessing of knowing the God of Israel. When her husband died she became emotional and wept, but walked away.

Naomi, the mother of the two boys, represents the backslider, who knew the Lord at one time in her life but slowly slipped away.

Ruth is a picture of a new believer. She was touched by the life and testimony of Naomi (even though she had backslidden) and gave up all to follow to an enemy country where she met her Boaz, married him and had a baby, Obed. Her name is mentioned in the genealogy of our Lord Jesus Christ in the Gospel of Matthew 1.

So...which of these 3 women do you identify with today?

So What Do You Think?

Thoughts to Ponder by Eleanor

Wait and Trust

If your theology doesn't match up with your reality, just wait and trust.

Abide

Sometimes we abide more in the fruit than in the vine.

Life a Vapor

But vapor channelled and controlled can pull a locomotive.

Sperm

God speaks to sperm. You are a "handmade" product of your Creator. He needed a special sperm to make YOU.

Male and Female

The largest cell in the body is the female egg. The smallest cell in the body is the male sperm.

Icy Road

What can keep you from slipping on an icy road is carrying a heavy load! Heavy loads in our lives are God's gift to help us walk steadily for Him.

Offence

Lowliness of mind will never GIVE offense. Meekness of mind will never TAKE offense.

Stars and Sand

Did you know that there are ten times more stars in the sky than all the sand on ALL the seashores?

Fine and Finer

God makes a rough man fine and a fine man finer.

Anger

Anger is only one letter short of Danger.

Head and Heart

To handle yourself use your head. To handle others use your heart!

True Friends

Many people will walk in and out of your life. True friends will leave footprints in your heart.

Betrayed

If someone betrays you once, it's his fault; if he betrays you twice, it's yours!

Great Minds

Great minds discuss ideas. Average minds discuss events. But small minds discuss people!

Birds

God gives every bird it's food, but he doesn't throw it into the nest.

Losing

He who loses money, loses much. He who loses friends, loses more. But he who loses faith, loses ALL

Beauty

Beautiful young people are acts of nature, but beautiful old people are works of art.

Mistakes

Learn from the mistakes of others, you can't live long enough to make them all yourself.

The Tongue

The tongue weights practically nothing, but few people can hold it.

The Bible

The first word in the Bible is "In." The last word in the Bible is "Amen."

Surprise

Words you won't find in the Bible are Trinity, Rapture, Smile and Evangelism.

Toxic People

God's shortcut to make us disciplined and godly is toxic people in our lives.

Trees

Trees lose their leaves in the Fall but they don't panic because they know spring is coming and more leaves will grow.

Champions

Champions are not made in the fight, they are only recognized there!
Joe Frazier

His Joy

For the joy set before Him, He endured the cross despising the shame (Hebrews 12:2) to have you and me in His life.

Circumcision

Why did God command it on that part of a man's body? Because that is the organ on which He reproduces Himself.

He is reminded daily to live for the Lord and raise his children for Him!

Bumps

Bumps are what we climb on
Warren Wiersbe

Obedience

Delayed obedience is really disobedience, but instant obedience is Faith in Action.

Now

Now Faith is, if it isn't NOW, it isn't Faith!

Now faith is the assurance of things hoped for, the conviction of things not seen.

—Hebrews 11:1

Death of The Wicked

God has no pleasure in the death of the wicked! (2 Peter 3:9, Titus 2:11).

Yet it pleased the Lord to bruise Him, Jesus (Isaiah 53:10) because it redeemed us to a Holy God.

Impatience

Whenever we are impatient, we create an Ishmael.

Fear

He who is heard, held, and hidden by the Lord need not fear anything.

The Holy Spirit

He who has the Holy Spirit in his heart, and the Scriptures in his hands, has all he needs.

A. McClaren

God's Word

How can we afford not to be in God's Word?

H. Hendricks

Alone

Great eagles fly alone. Great lions hunt alone. Great souls walk alone, alone with God.

L. Ravenhill

Forgive

We never so touch the ocean of God's love, as when we forgive and love our enemies.

Corrie Ten Boom

Overcomers

Believers are either overcome because of their unbelief, or Overcomers because of their faith.

Warren Wiersbe

The Ten Commandments

Did you know that God keeps His commandments Himself towards you?

Peace

At peace with the Father and at war with His kids? It cannot be!

John Flavel

Temptations

Are all around us, and so is the Grace of God.

Unknown

Machines

A machine can do the work, but only life can bear fruit for God

Andrew Murray

God's Workman

I infer that losses and disappointments are God's workman in our lives.

Sam Rutherford

God's Purpose

God permits no suffering, no trials without a purpose, even though that purpose may be hidden from us

Frank Retief

Placed on Earth

You were placed on earth to know God; everything else is secondary!

Greg Laurie

A Quadriplegic

For a quadriplegic like me, it's a heartwarming assurance; it's a wonderful feeling to know that somebody's gonna carry Me.

Joni Fareckson Tada

The Atonement

The Atonement is the real reason for the incarnation.

James Montgomery Boice

Evangelism

Evangelism is a command—Go into all the world and preach the Gospel to every creature—but it is also a gift from God. Are you using it?

Choosing Our Sins

We can choose our sins, but never the consequences!

Curious

I don't have any talents, I'm just forever curious.

Albert Einstein

Gateway to Joy

Everything, if given to God, can become your gateway to Joy.

Elizabeth Elliot

Joy

Only to sit and think of God. Oh, what a joy this is.

F. W. Faber

Forgiveness

Perhaps the most glorious word in the English language is Forgiveness.

Billy Graham

Surrender

If you don't surrender to Christ, you surrender to chaos"

E. Stanley Jones

Lesson and Tests

In school, the lessons come first, then the tests. In Christ, the test comes first, then the lessons.

David Jeremiah

So What Do You Think?

Created and Born

God Created man in His own image.

—Genesis 1:27

For unto us a child is born.

—Isaiah 9:6

Adam was created a full-grown man, but our Lord Jesus Christ was born an infant, and became a man.

So Adam never had to grow up. He had no idea what it would be like to be a child, and experience all the childhood challenges.

Is that why he was a bad influence on his first son Cain, who killed his brother, Abel, over religion? After all, Adam the father, sinned and disobeyed the Word of God, by eating from the forbidden tree. So, Cain must have learned, that it is okay to disobey God. "Why should I obey the laws of God, if Dad didn't?" Cain just followed in his footsteps (Genesis 1:1-18).

Adams' disobedience created a whole race of sinners, rich and poor sinners, young and old ones, and we all have a nature that is capable of disobeying God. That is why we all need a Savior to redeem us back to God.

Unlike Adam who was created a full-grown man, our Lord Jesus Christ was born into this world an infant and he grew up in favor with God and Man. He knew what childhood was like, and he knew what being an adult was like. He is therefore able to be our perfect

Savior and our perfect example in how to love, serve and obey a Holy God. He is able to be everybody's Savior, young and old, rich and poor...all people!

Adam is called the "first Adam" in that he is the head of the human race of sinners. But Christ is called the "second Adam", in that He is the head of a new spiritual race, believers, redeemed by his death (1 Corinthians 15:45-49).

When we accept Jesus' death for us, we become "born again" believers. We become His Bride, to be loved and adored by our spiritual Bridegroom. We can have and enjoy A Divine Romance with Jesus (Ephesians 5:22-23).

So What Do You Think?

Cain and Abel

> Cain spoke to Abel his brother. And when they were in the field, Cain rose up against his brother Abel and killed him. Then the Lord said to Cain, "Where is Abel your brother?" He said, "I do not know; am I my brother's keeper?"
>
> —Genesis 4:8-9

God had said "If you eat of that tree, you shall surely die." But they probably had no idea what that meant, and what death would look like. Abel was the first person to die in the Garden of Eden.

So here lay the dead body of Abel! Adam and Eve must have picked it up, shook it, maybe rubbed it, brought water to help him drink it, talk to him, kissed him and hold him, but he was lifeless in their arms, never to be alive again.

Perhaps they thought he is just in a deep sleep and tomorrow he would be with them again. However, the next day his body began to deteriorate and have an odor. How did they bury him? We don't know, but it must have been a terrible time for them. They must have been shocked, puzzled, confused and angry with God.

We really don't know any of the details. Maybe they were used to animals dying, but never thought people would die the same way.

Anyway, just in case you may think that this is just a story in the book of Genesis, let me remind you, that every time you pass a cemetery, just remember, it is a reminder for all of us that, God was not kidding when He said "You shall surely die" (Genesis 2:17).

So What Do You Think?

Sports: Acceptable Aggression and Violence

Have you ever watched a game and realized that the people on the field are literally brutally beating each other up over a ball? We sit and watch it with no thought that some of these players may end up with life-long injuries.

If all this violence would happen in a park or on a street, the Police would come and break up the fight. Some might even be arrested and put in jail.

So, why is this aggression and violence in a game so acceptable with many of us? Sports seems to be such a popular pastime, and the players and spectators all seem to be so caught up with it, love and enjoy it?

Is it because, (the Bible is always right) since Adam and Eve sinned in the Garden of Eden, we have an evil, aggressive and violent nature, like the devil, but we harness it with education, refinement, culture and putting on aires?

However, when we become born again believers, Jesus Christ and the indwelling Holy Spirit, shape us into Christlike beings, that is, we become gentle, forgiving, loving, and non violent people.

In sports, aggression and violence is acceptable. It gives the "Old Nature," which we all inherited from Adam, permission to "let it all out" without being arrested.

> Put off the old nature which is corrupt, and be renewed in the spirit of your mind, and put on the new nature."
>
> —Ephesians 4:22-24

Put off your old self, which belongs to your former manner of life and is corrupt through deceitful desires, and to be renewed in the spirit of your minds, and to put on the new self, created after the likeness of God in true righteousness and holiness.

Interesting, isn't it?

So What Do You Think?

Being Single

For your Maker is your husband, the Lord of Hosts is his name...

—Isaiah 54:5

So you're single! It's tough being One in a world of Twos! God said in Genesis 2:18, "It is not good that the man should be alone; I will make him a helper fit for him."

At this point in your life, God hasn't come through for you in this area. Has He forgotten you, or does He have a different plan for your life?

The Bible calls unmarried women "virgins" because God is of the opinion that if you do not belong to a man, you belong strictly to Him! You are His Bride, The Bride of Christ, to be loved, cherished and adored.

There is nothing wrong with wanting to be married. It is a natural desire.

But since "a Mr. Wonderful" may not be on your horizon right now, take advantage of this alone-time, by taking care of the things of the Lord while you are waiting, and also take very good care of yourself.

Single women ought to be the most consecrated women in the Church. Instead of singles being envious of married women, the married women ought to be jealous of the singles who have all the time in the world to live for, and worship the Lord without distractions. It has to be a choice singles have to make, that the will of God is always the best for us, and that includes marriage or singleness.

While married women depend on their husbands, single women learn to be completely dependent on the Lord. A married woman may have a husband who can do some things, but God can do everything.

What a privilege to be married to Him. God told Joel:

> And upon the handmaids, (single people) will I pour out my Spirit.
>
> —Joel 2:29

God has a very special blessing for the woman who Is free to seek Him.

A woman's prayer life should explode into miracles for her, and those all around her.

So What Do You Think?

The Altars of God

> Even the sparrow finds a home, and the swallow a nest for herself, where she may lay her young, at your altars, O Lord of Hosts, my King and my God.
>
> —Psalm 84:3

That is also the best place for our children to be—on the Altar of God!

How much we can learn from little birds and from nature.

We worry, we struggle in prayer and sacrifice over our children. We work hard to bring them up right, but all we really need to do is to give them to God, who gave them to us in the first place. Laying them on yhe Altar of God, by faith, is the best and safest place for them.

This will also bring peace to us, no matter what comes into their lives. We need to be steadfast in faith trusting the Lord to work in their lives. If they should fall away from the faith, as they grow into adult life, we need to trust the Lord that He will so work in their lives to bring them back to Himself.

This also means that when they become of age, we need to keep our hands off the work of God in their lives. Actually, from the moment they are conceived your children are not yours but the Lord's. You'll be especially aware of this if you dedicated them to Him They are just loaned to you for a short time to raise them, as best you know how.

I like the verse about committing anything, and especially our children, to the Lord.

> For I know whom I have believed, and I am convinced that he is able to guard until that day what [our children] has been entrusted to me.
>
> —2 Timothy 1:12

So dear parents, don't lose your peace when your children don't turn out the way you hoped they would. You gave them to the Lord, now He will mold and teach them, no matter how they turn out! Trust Him!

So What Do You Think?

The Next Time You Feel Like God Can't Use You

Just remember some of these people, from the Bible, who failed terribly...

Noah was a drunk.
Abraham was too old.
Isaac was a daydreamer.
Jacob was a liar.
Leah had weak eyes.
Joseph was abused.
Moses had a stuttering problem.
Gideon was afraid.
Samson was a womanizer.
Rahab was a prostitute.
Jeremiah and Timothy were too young.
David had an affair and was a murderer.
Elijah was suicidal.
Isaiah preached naked.
Jonah ran from God.
Naomi was an angry widow.
Job went bankrupt.
John the Baptist ate bugs.
Peter denied Jesus three times.
Martha worried about everything.
The Samaritan woman was immoral.

Zachaeus was too short.
The disciples fell asleep while praying.
Paul was too religious.
Timothy had an ulcer.
And Lazarus was dead!

So there...no more excuses now!

The Lord used all these people, after they had great failure in their lives. God forgave them and used them in a mighty way. So will it be with you and me, when we confess and agree with God about our shortcomings and sins.

> There is therefore NOW no condemnation to them who are Christ Jesus, who walk not after the flesh, but after the Spirit.
>
> —Romans 8:1

So What Do You Think?

JOSEPH IN PRISON

> When Potiphar heard the words of his wife [that Joseph acted inappropriately with her] that his anger was kindled.
>
> —Genesis 39:19

So who was Potiphar angry with, was it Joseph or his wife? He must have known his wife, what kind of a woman she was. She probably tried the same thing with other men, that she tried with Joseph. When they didn't respond to her seduction, she would tell her husband that, they started the whole thing.

I think Potiphar was angry with his wife, and not with Joseph. He knew what kind of righteous man Joseph was. He saw evidence of this in his skill in managing his household. Joseph was an honorable man, and Potiphar put him in charge of all the affairs of his whole house.

Potiphar was the executioner, so why did he not put him to death? It was to save face! Maybe Potiphar wanted Joseph to "take care of his prison!" Joseph did such a fine job in taking care of his house, now he wanted him to do the same thing in his prison.

Joseph took it all from the Lord and never complained, but trusted every event in his life, as from the Hand of God. What a man of faith he was. We can all learn from him.

When Joseph got to be the Prime Minister, just think, Mrs. Potiphar had to be under his control. We never read that he got even with her.

So What Do You Think?

God's Two Tablets

> Before I was afflicted I went astray, but now I keep your word... Therefore I love your commandments above gold, above fine gold.
>
> —Psalm 119:67 & 127

Are you bored with life? Do you lack purpose, and you wonder why you are here at this time in history? Are you stressed out, sick and tired of it all? Here is the remedy...

Take two of God's Tablets every morning and have a visit with Dr. Jesus Christ, your Great Physician!

> He sent His Word and healed them, and delivered them from their destruction.
>
> —Psalm 107:20

> He forgives all our iniquities, and heals all our diseases, who redeems your life from destruction.
>
> —Psalm 103:3

> Showing mercy to thousands, to those who love me, and keep my Commandments.
>
> —Exodus 20:6

So What Do You Think?

The Burning Bush

The bush burned with fire, and the bush was not consumed.

—Exodus 3:2

At the age of eighty Moses began his greatest ministry. Up to the age of forty, Moses wanted to deliver the Israelites from Egypt, who were in bondage close to 430 years. However, it was a long process for God to prepare a deliverer to do this great job.

When Moses was born, the king had decided at that time, that the Hebrew people were growing in multitude and strength, and so he commanded the midwives to kill all baby boys but keep the girls alive.

Moses' mother was hiding him, but after three months she could no longer do so. So, I'm sure after much prayer, she built a small ark and dropped it into the river. As the king's daughter went to bathe, she saw this odd-looking basket floating near her, and had it brought to her. When she opened the basket, we read "the baby wept." It touched her heart, and he became her son. She called the baby Moses, "because I drew him out of the water."

The king's daughter took the baby to Moses' mother who nursed and cared for him, but at a certain age Pharaoh's daughter brought him back to be raised in the Palace. There he was to probably be groomed to be the next king. I'm sure his parents hoped he would someday delivery the Israelites out of Egypt.

At the age of forty, Moses murdered one of the Egyptians and had to flee Egypt. He lived in the desert for forty years taking care of sheep.

It is interesting to think of it this way. For the first forty years of Moses' life, he learned to be somebody. Then for the next forty years he learned to be nobody. Now at eighty, Moses lost all self-confidence and was now ready to rely wholly on the Lord.

While keeping the sheep, Moses saw a bush on fire, but it was not consumed. A voice said "Moses, Moses, take off your shoes because you are on holy ground" (Exodus 3:5). God spoke to him out of the burning bush telling him to deliver the Israelites by speaking to Pharaoh, to let the Israelites go.

At this point, he did not stay and pray or built an altar to commemorate this exciting event. He obeyed the voice of the Lord. He was now ready to lead the nation of Israel out of Egypt.

God prepares each of us for the ministry he has for us to do. What are you going to do?

So What Do You Think?

I And My Father Are One

I am in my Father, and you are in me and I am in you.

—John 14:20

God is a Trinity and so are You!

He represents the Father, the Son and the Holy Spirit. You and I are a Trinity as well. We are a Body, a Soul and a Spirit. Those three need to be in total agreement for us to be healthy, happy and useful human beings!

I have always wondered what the Star of David represented, and no Jewish man or woman, or even a Rabbi, could tell me what it meant. They all told me that it was a mystical symbol. So I asked God to tell me and He did.

Teaching Jewish Bible classes in New Jersey, the Lord gave me a beautiful answer, the Star of David. It represents the Jewish faith. But what does it mean? God showed me that is a Christian symbol, not a Jewish one.

You see, it is two triangles intersecting, one points down and the other one up. It represents the Holy Trinity reaching down, and our human trinity reaching up!

So the Star of David is a visible, tangible symbol of our union with the Lord. The cross is really a Jewish symbol in that it represents the blood on the doorpost at the time of the Passover (Exodus 12).

It represents the arrangement of the furniture in the Tabernacle (Exodus 25-31).

It explains the meaning of the Snake on the Pole (Numbers 21).

All of these things foreshadow the coming of the Messiah, and how He would die on a Cross for our sins. The furniture in the Tabernacle was arranged in the shape of a cross. The Snake on the Pole was for healing. Everyone who was bidden by the snake, if they just looked on the snake, they were healed.

So it is today. All we need to do is by faith look at the Cross of Calvary, believe that Jesus died there for us, make it personal, and we will be saved, born again and made whole.

So What Do You Think?

THEY SAW HIS NAIL-PIERCED HANDS

> When he was at table with them, he took the bread and blessed and broke it and gave it to them. And their eyes were opened, and they recognized him. And he vanished from their sight.
>
> —Luke 24:30-31

After His resurrection, the disciples were puzzled as to what actually took place.

In this passage, we see two of them walking home from Jerusalem, talking about all that had taken place and how Jesus was crucified. We read that a "stranger" began to walk with them and talking about the events of the day. While the two were confused and sad, Jesus, He pretended to be the stranger, explained to them how that in the Old Testament it was predicted that Christ would suffer and be put to death and rise up from the dead. They didn't know that it was Jesus in His resurrection that was speaking with them.

They invited him into their home for supper, but He acted as if He was going on.

Because they insisted that He come in, He accepted their invitation. It was at the table, when He gave thanks and broke the bread, that they suddenly realized who He was. It was indeed Jesus risen from the dead.

Could it be that as he broke the bread, they saw His nail pierced hands? It was then that they realized that it was true, Jesus did rise from the dead and has appeared unto many, including them. Even though it was probably late in the evening, they rushed back to Jerusalem to tell the disciples.

Our Lord Jesus will make Himself known in our lives too. If He seems far away from you now, just wait in His presence and He will make Himself known to you also, in His Time, so wait!

So What Do You Think?

You Are Worth It

...for the joy that was set before him endured the cross, despising the shame, and is seated at the right hand of the throne of God.

Hebrews 12:2

Our Lord Jesus was not occupied with the present moment of pain and ultimate crucifixion, but He looked ahead to the joy that was to be His at the end of the pain an suffering. He knew that His Father had a good and eternal purpose in it all.

We need to learn to do that in our lives too, when trials come our way. It has been said....

Never judge a tragedy at the moment it is happening.

Anonymous

Our loving Heavenly Father has a plan and purpose, and we need to trust Him.

Champions are not made in the ring; they are only recognized there.

Joe Frazier
Professional Boxer from 1965 to 1981

So it is in our daily disciplined life that we develop a champion life style.

Jesus looked at the Cross and then He looked at you and said It's worth it.

So What Do You Think?

MOSES BROKE THE TEN COMMANDMENTS

> As soon as he came near the camp and saw the calf and the dancing, Moses' anger burned hot, and he threw the tablets out of his hands and broke them at the foot of the mountain.
>
> —Exodus 32:19

> Moses did not know that his face shone because he had been talking with God.
>
> —Exodus 34:29

The first time Moses came down from the mountain with the first set of the 10 Commandments, he broke them in anger when he saw what the people had done to build a golden calf and to worship it. Moses was up in the mountain talking with the Lord to get the 10 Commandments. Since he was gone forty days, the people were restless and wondered if he would ever come back.

So they asked Aaron to make them a god to worship. He said, bring me all the gold earrings. He melted them and formed a golden calf and threw it into the fire.

The funniest verse in the Bible for me is the following. It sounds something like "The dog ate my homework."

> So they gave [the gold] to me, and I threw it into the fire, and out came this calf."
>
> —Exodus 32:24

Moses went back on the mountain to meet God, and get a second set of Commandments. When he came down to meet the people, his face was shining. Why didn't it shine the first trip to the mountain?

Because this time, he learned the character of God, His mercy, compassion on sinners, His great love for fallen man, and His forgiveness. He came to know more of the character of God, in that He forgave the Israelites for their idol worship.

So What Do You Think?

God is Lonely Without You

Adam where are you?

—Genesis 3:9

For the Son of man came to seek and to save that which is lost.

—Luke 19:10

I the Lord your God am a jealous God.

—Exodus 20:5

Did you ever think of this? God is lonely without YOU!

Throughout the Bible, we see how anxious God has been to draw people to Himself. He Is jealous when we worship someone or some things more than Him.

Why? He has myriads of angels who worship Him, so why seek you and me?

He created man to have close fellowship, intimacy and a daily walk with us. Obviously, He does not have the same kind of fellowship with angels.

How humbling this is, and how precious to think that I can make Him happy today by my worship, love and devotion.

How little we realize the need our Lord has to be loved, believed, adored and worshipped. The whole story of our Lord Jesus being crucified on Calvary's cross, is for us to be reunited with Him.

Let's give Him our best today!

So What Do You Think?

More Than a Conqueror

In all these things, we are more than conquerors through Him who loved us.

—Romans 8:37

We believers are conquerors in any battle because our Lord Jesus Christ has freed us from the power of sin, when He paid for our sins on the Cross of Calvary. So how can we be more than conquerors? Here is an example...

It is like the boxing champion who won the fight and arrives home, wounded, bandaged up, but holding the prize of $100,000 in his hand. He gives the check to his proud and adoring wife, who was watching the fight on TV and was so proud that her husband won the fight. She dances around the room waving the check in the air.

So, he is the conqueror of the fight, but she is more than a conqueror, why?

Because, she holds the prize, without the wounds!

So, my friend, you are more than a conqueror, when you have made the Lord Jesus Christ your personal Savior and Lord. He is the conqueror when He died for us on the cross of Calvary. He won the fight and had wounds to prove it, but you and I are more than conquerors, because we have all the benefits of His

Death for us, but no wounds!

Hallelujah, what a Savior!

So What Do You Think?

This Brings The Book to a Close

This brings *The Divine Romance With Jesus* devotional to a close.

Some pages are not directly related to romance, but I have included them to help you realize how loved you are, no matter how the Lord is molding you through difficult circumstances right now in your life.

I trust you have enjoyed the thoughts on these pages, and have drawn closer to your heavenly Bridegroom. Remember, you are so loved, both like a much-loved child, and a Bride who is adored by her Lover and Bridegroom.

Your heavenly Bridegroom has great plans for your life, as you mature in Him. Be faithful in your times with Him, spend lots of time in His Word, prayer and meditation. Enjoy solitude in His presence, and be on the lookout to serve Him every day with boldness and joy. He has kind. loving and passionate thoughts toward you.

> For I know the plans I have for you, declares the Lord, plans of peace and not for evil, to give you a future and a hope.
>
> —Jeremiah 29:11

I'd love to hear from you! Feel free to write to me at edi14@verizon.net.

Be happy gossiping the Gospel!

About the Author

Born in New Jersey, speaker, author, and WWII survivor Eleanor Isaacson was raised till age thirteen in East Germany. Returning to the USA with neither English nor family, she overcame every obstacle to graduate with a double Bachelor's Degree magna cum laude, become a successful business entrepreneur, and marry renowned scientist Dr. Robert Isaacson. She is also a competitive ballroom dancer with more than 100 first-place wins.

Eleanor has been an inspirational speaker for more than forty years throughout the United States. She was voted "The Speaker of the Year" for the past five years in Lancaster County. She was also awarded an honorary Doctoral Degree from Lancaster Bible College in 2017.

You can contact Eleanor at edi14@verizon.net.

Read Eleanor's Award-Winning Story!

Dancing from Darkness: A WWII Survivor's Journey to Light, Life, and Redemption

2018 Memoir of the Year by American Writers and Speakers Association

Abandoned as a toddler in Nazi Germany, American-born Eleanor Isaacson survived bombings, starvation, Russian occupation, and a stint as a child smuggler—all before reaching her teens.

Escaping just as the Iron Curtain clashed shut, Eleanor soon discovered that "the land of the free" held as much pain and rejection as the life she'd escaped. Deafness and solitude would become the catalyst leading to glorious womanhood, the love of her life, and the beauty of dance.

In the process, she would discover that the "invisible Friend" whose presence alone had kept a lost child sane had other names—heavenly Father, loving God, Prince of Peace.

A true story too implausible for fiction with every element of a big screen epic—war, danger, starvation, villains, romance, rags-to-riches triumph—along with the most delightful of heroines.

Another Book by Eleanor

The Invisible Presence: Meditations to Help You Praise, Pray, Think, and Smile

The Invisible Presence has its inception from Dr. Eleanor Isaacson's award-winning top-selling personal survival story *Dancing from Darkness*. Abandoned as a toddler in Nazi Germany, American-born Eleanor survived bombings, starvation, Russian occupation, and a stint as a child smuggler—all before reaching her teens. Throughout it was the Invisible Presence who made Himself known to her that kept a lost child sane. A Presence she would eventually come to know by other names—heavenly Father, loving God, Prince of Peace.

Since Eleanor began sharing her story, listeners and readers alike have begged to know more about her encounter with the Invisible Presence and how they too might find Him. Responding to those pleas, *The Invisible Presence* is a compilation of meditations and humorous thoughts on God, faith, Scripture, and Eleanor's own spiritual journey intended to make the reader praise, pray, think, and smile.

Another Book by Eleanor

Sitting on God's Lap...Listening. More Meditations About the Invisible Presence

Dr. Eleanor Isaacson was born in New Jersey but at age two was abandoned to relatives in Germany just before war broke out. She survived the terrors of the Nazi Regime, the bombings, the starvation, the American and Russian occupation, and became a child smuggler at age 11.

Throughout the war, Eleanor felt there was Someone invisible who was watching and protecting her. She found peace and safety by imagining she was sitting on His lap... listening and feeling the warmth of His arms around her.

She returned to the USA alone at the age of 13, overcoming every obstacle to graduate with a magna cum laude bachelor's degree, become a successful business entrepreneur, and marry scientist Dr. Robert Isaacson.

What joy to find later in life that God had been that invisible Someone, her spiritual dad with a purpose in keeping her alive. He allowed all the pain and suffering of her life to draw her to Himself. Since Eleanor began sharing her story in her book Dancing from Darkness, readers have begged to know more about her encounters with God. They too want to know how they might get to know God in such an intimate and personal way.

Invite Eleanor to Speak

As a presenter and confident speaker, Eleanor Isaacson is available to speak to various groups, including schools, on a variety of topics including:

- Finding God in Nazi Germany
- The Educational System under the Nazi Regime
- The Christmas Tradition—Why we Do It the Way We Do
- Positive Attitudes and Nutritional Helps that Can Help You to Be Your Best at Any Age
- How to Be a Vibrant Senior
- Widowhood—the Next Stage of the Adventure
- How to Break Generational Bondages—Dealing with Difficult Parents as an Adult

You can contact Eleanor at edi14@verizon.net

Made in the USA
Middletown, DE
12 November 2023